FREQUENT QUESTIONS POSED TO A RIDE-SHARE DRIVER

WILLIAM MAICHEL

WESTBOW PRESS®
A DIVISION OF THOMAS NELSON & ZONDERVAN

WestBow Press books may be ordered through booksellers or by contacting:

WestBow Press
A Division of Thomas Nelson & Zondervan
1663 Liberty Drive
Bloomington, IN 47403
www.westbowpress.com
1 (866) 928-1240

ISBN: 978-1-5127-7396-5 (sc)
ISBN: 978-1-5127-7395-8 (e)

Library of Congress Control Number: 2017901415

Print information available on the last page.

WestBow Press rev. date: 02/08/2017

INTRODUCTION

At the time this book was being written, I had been a ride-share driver for one year. Several months in, I started noticing the questions riders asked were the same trip after trip … reworded a little, but still the same. Why would they ask these questions? Are they motivated out of uneasiness due to lack of conversation? Are the passengers curious to know the driver's story?

What if a book existed that could answer some of these questions? The answers for the preceding questions have been left blank. The owner of the book can customize the answers for his or her own story.

CONTENTS

CHAPTER 1

JOB

How long have you been a ride-share driver?

What did you do before driving?

Why did you start driving?

Is this your full-time job?

Do you enjoy driving?

What do you like best about this job?

Do you have any interesting stories?

CHAPTER 2

CAR

What make and model of car is this?

What's the mileage like?

* Is this car a standard … are you shifting?

* Usually asked in connection with brake-shifting on a hybrid or electric vehicle.

When did you buy your car?

Did you buy the car specifically for this type of work?

Do you like your car?

Why do you wear gloves?

Have you experienced any issues with your car?

How many miles does your car have?

How well does your car handle on snow or ice?

CHAPTER 3

PERSONAL QUESTIONS

The questions in chapter 3 could be considered very personal. Please consider your answers carefully before recording them in the book.

Are you married?

Do you have children?

What are your political views?

What is your family background?

What are your spiritual beliefs?

Do you live in a house or an apartment?

CHAPTER 4

ADVICE FOR PASSENGERS

Be respectful to your driver and the driver's property. Drivers use their personal vehicles for ride-share services.

The driver may have rules regarding what is allowed or not allowed in his or her car:

> Carrying open containers of alcohol in the car may be legal in one area but not legal in other areas. One doesn't necessarily know the route or municipal boundaries a driver may have to traverse to complete the trip.
>
> The prohibition of food or drink in the vehicle usually stems from past experiences when passengers left messes behind that required a professional cleaning service.

"In everything treat others the same
way you want them to treat you."
—Matthew 7:12 (AMP)

ABOUT THE AUTHOR

William is from Kansas City with over a year of experience as a ride-share driver.